i'll wait in the car
dogs along for the ride

marcie jan bronstein

SELLERS
PUBLISHING

To Alan and Noah … with me every step along the way

— mjb

Published by Sellers Publishing, Inc.
Copyright © 2008 Marcie Jan Bronstein
All rights reserved.

Sellers Publishing, Inc.
161 John Roberts Rd.
South Portland, Maine 04106
For ordering information:
(800) 625-3386 toll free
Visit our Web site: www.rsvp.com • E-mail: rsp@rsvp.com

President & Publisher: Ronnie Sellers
Publishing Director: Robin Haywood
Managing Editor: Mary Baldwin
Senior Editor: Megan Hiller
Assistant Production Editor: Charlotte Smith

ISBN: 13: 978-1-56906-993-6

10 9 8 7 6 5 4 3 2 1

Printed and bound in China.

foreword

I am in awe of these photos — and the short, sweet, funny words that go with them — because they are so achingly beautiful, while also giving us a window into the soul of dogs. These images capture the devotion and patience of our canine friends, along with the mysterious way that driving out into the world with us, and then being left in the car to await our return, cements our special bond with them. Marcie Jan Bronstein understands how sharing our world in the car captures the essence of the way that our pooches are interlocked with us — it is a deep and abiding expression of their patient belief that we will be back.

All three of my large dogs go with me in the car anytime that weather permits (meaning below 68 degrees and above 32), and I swear it is their favorite place to be — more than the beach or a hike on a trail. The impending possibility of a car ride elicits pure joy — my youngest rescued Weimaraner, Teddy, appears to do cartwheels at the prospect. But since they rarely have a chance to get out of the car (there is hardly any establishment that welcomes a cumulative 300 pounds of dogs), they are often doing what this gorgeous little book celebrates: waiting in the car.

Marcie has caught in images and phrases the dignity, delight, and steadfast devotion of these dogs who remain in the car, holding down the fort, waiting until their human reappears. I have always known how deliriously happy it makes dogs to be included in a car outing, but until this gem of a book I hadn't stopped to realize how waiting in the car is in itself an act of faith, trust, and unconditional love.

This little book is eloquent and elegant — a wonderful gift, but I hope you will treat yourself to it first. Anyone who loves dogs needs to have this reminder of why, right on their shelf.

Tracie Hotchner
author of The Dog Bible *and*
host of Dog Talk, *the radio show*

introduction

It all began when I spotted a fine white poodle in a well used pick-up truck.

Ten years and hundreds of photographs later, I'm still captivated by the ubiquitous, infinitely diverse world of dogs waiting in cars. And it's no small wonder. These faithful friends are uniquely and beautifully engaged in an act most humans haven't the patience or attention to experience fully: the act of waiting.

As with all long-term studies, some universal truths emerged. Most importantly, I found that dogs in cars are truly pleased to be where they are. There's no doubt about it, from a dog's perspective a ride in a car is a treat and waiting in the car is an adventure. Dogs in the parking lot waiting for their owners are there because they love the person they are waiting for and they love to be in the car.

It doesn't take much imagination, upon seeing a dog in a car, to know that just a few moments earlier someone asked that dog, in a sing-song voice no doubt:

"Do you want to go for a ride?"

marcie jan bronstein

There are dogs waiting alone,

dogs waiting with friends,

dogs waiting with relatives,

and puppies learning to wait.

There are big dogs,

small dogs,

and dogs beyond description.

There are old dogs,

new dogs,

and dogs that seem ageless.

But there is no correlation between the look of a dog and the look of a car.

There are so many breeds of dogs
and so many kinds of cars,
but there are also
so many styles of waiting.

There's the classic,

the nouveau,

the retro,

and the *Waiting for Godot.*

By the time you see a dog in a car,
he will have already detected you . . .

and sized you up from head to toe.

Some dogs in cars are used to posing for the camera.

Some might offer their best side.

Others who are shy may be
feeling exposed,

but all dogs waiting in cars should
be given their space.

One can't help but wonder if for some dogs
waiting in cars is a mystical experience

or simply one of life's great pleasures.

Because that's what waiting is all about.

It's a quiet adventure

with limitless space and time . . .

a collection of tiny moments,

a bridge between reason and rhyme.

Dogs seem to know that waiting is whatever one wishes it to be.

A time to see

and be seen,

or to hide

and to dream...

beyond the parking lot.

Dogs waiting in cars may be sleepy,
but they won't go to sleep.

And dogs don't need to read or
listen to the radio,

because they always have
something on their minds.

Dogs waiting in cars are caretakers,
guarding the family car

while searching for signs of friend or foe.

After all, they are so much more than
simply the pets of their owners.
They are companions, infinitely patient,

and dependents,
eyes peeled for the first glimpse
of their owners.

At times they are chauffeurs,

keeping the driver's seat warm

and taking their job rather seriously.

Rain or shine, our dogs are waiting
and watching

with their finely tuned senses

and their immeasurable sense of loyalty.

So keep your eyes on the dogs.

You'll see that the act of waiting
is profound and noble,

steadfast,

and sincere.

And you will fully understand
why dogs are called faithful friends.